COPYRIGHT

Sparkle At Every Step by Lesley D. Nurse New York, NY © 2021
Lesley Nurse. All rights reserved. No portion of this book may be
reproduced in any form without permission from the publisher
except as permitted by U.S. copyright law. Illustrated by Lesley D.
Nurse.
ISBN: 9780578323732
Third Edition
Printed in the United States of America

INTRODUCTION

···

Dear Star, I created this book to share that
it is up to you to sparkle at every step.
Sparkle at every step is about how you see life,
no matter how much it may go up, down, and around!
You have a voice, you have courage, talent,
and so much more to offer to the world.
Here are some powerful words that will give you energy
no matter how you feel, just like life.
May you always remember that
your power is still within and belongs to you!

Don't be afraid of the dark.

That's the only way you will see the stars.

There is no name they can call you
that can define you unless you allow it to.

It is better to be a good friend

than a pretend friend.

STEP 4

Don't be afraid to let the world

see you shine brightly.

STEP 5

This world is big enough for you
and me and ours to share in peace.

STEP 6

It is okay to cry.

But don't forget to laugh afterward.

If you focus on the lesson
instead of the pain of the lesson.
Then you will find the blessing.

STEP 8

You are so special for so many reasons
that I lost count.

STEP 9

Be different.

It's who you are.

When you take pride
in doing a good job
with small things,
you will do an even greater
job with bigger things.

When someone tries to
pick you apart,
that means they feel
apart on the inside.

You are God's

one-of-a-kind work of art.

Your hair is beautiful,
no matter the size or the feel.

Your skin is part of you,
not all of you.
It's what's inside of you
that makes - you.

God made you different
because he knew the world
needed someone like you.

Don't let anyone make you feel
bad for feeling so good.

STEP 17

Never be afraid to reach

for the stars.

You can go as far as you want to go,

as long as you close your eyes and

dream it.

STEP 19

When you listen well when other
people speak,
other people will listen well
when you speak.

STEP 20

God loves a lending hand,
so lend a hand to someone else
who needs it.

If someone tries to feed you meanness,

don't take a bite.

STEP 22

No one can rock your special style

better than you.

Failures will always come
with losses and lessons.

STEP 24

Don't be hard on yourself
when things seem hard to do.

One day your parents will need you,

the same way that you need them today.

No fancy things can ever put into words

the joy that you bring.

Sometimes when you don't know what to do,

all you have to do is listen

to your inner light.

Check in with God sometimes,

not just to say please,

but to give thanks.

STEP 29

When you are kind to others,

others will be kind to you.

Always go with your heart,

not with the crowd.

Always give others joy,
but never let others take the joy
away from you.

REFLECTION CORNER

- Which Step made you smile the most today?

- When was the last time you helped someone else sparkle?

- What does your own light feel like when it shines?

SPARKLE ACTIVITY

Create Your Light Jar

Find a clean jar or cup. Each day, write one good thing you did or learned on a slip of paper and drop it inside.

By the end of 31 days, you'll have a jar full of light — proof that every day you sparkle in your own way.

(Encourage children to share one note each week with a classmate or family member.)

www.ingramcontent.com/pod-product-compliance
Lightning Source LLC
Chambersburg PA
CBHW061137030426
42334CB00003B/67

9780578323732